BEARER OF TWO PURE LIGHTS

UTHMAN
IBN AFFAN

FERRUH AKIN

TUGHRA
BOOKS

New Jersey

Copyright © 2022 by Tughra Books

25 24 23 22   3 4 5 6

All rights reserved. No part of this book may be reproduced
or transmitted in any form or by any means, electronic or
mechanical, including photocopying, recording or by any information storage and retrieval system without permission in
writing from the Publisher.

Published by
Tughra Books
335 Clifton Ave
Clifton, NJ 07011

www.tughrabooks.com

Library of Congress Cataloging-in-Publication
Data Available

ISBN: 978-1-59784-267-9

Translated by Abdullah Erdemli

TABLE OF CONTENTS

Chapter 1
Before Uthman's Conversion to Islam

Chapter 2
After He Embraced Islam

Chapter 3
His Caliphate

Appendices

*The man who had the honor of being the
son-in-law of the noble Prophet twice...
The third of the Four Rightly Guided Caliphs...
Admired for his modesty even by the angels...
Received promise of Paradise in his life...
The friend of the Messenger in Paradise...*

CHAPTER 1

Before Uthman's
Conversion to Islam

A Qur'anic verse written by Uthman ibn Affan
Topkapi Palace Museum, Inventory number 21/233

BEFORE UTHMAN'S CONVERSION TO ISLAM

His Birth and Name

He was born six years after Abraha headed with his army to Mecca to destroy the Ka'ba. Uthman was one of the first converts to Islam and became a Muslim through the guidance and encouragement of Abu Bakr.

His father Affan named him Uthman. His real birth occurred, however, after his *hijra* (migration) to Medina. In *hijra*, there was obedience to God's command, holiness, devotion, and self-sacrifice for God's sake. *Hijra* meant a rebirth of servanthood. Uthman was nicknamed Abu Abdullah, Abu Amr, and Abu Layla. His mother was Urwa bint Kariz and his grandmother,

Bayza, was also the aunt of the Prophet and the daughter of Abdul Muttalib. Therefore, Uthman was related to the Messenger of God.

Uthman was a tenderhearted, sweet-faced, and good-tempered person of a medium height. His face had slight traces of smallpox. His hair fell to his shoulders and he occasionally applied henna to his beard, which was quite large, bushy and brownish. He was a big-boned person with broad shoulders.

Uthman's Twin Sister

Uthman had a twin sister named Amina bint Affan. She was a hairdresser during the Age of Ignorance (*Jahiliya*). She and her mother did not convert to Islam until the conquest of Mecca, finally embarking on the savior ship captained by the Prophet. The rest of Uthman's brothers and sisters converted to Islam after them.

Uthman During the Age of Ignorance

Uthman was one of those rare persons who, during the dark days of the Age of Ignorance led a virtuous life, not indulging in the impurities of that time. He was one of the leaders of his society. His presence was felt through his generosity, soft words, civility, modesty, and a lifestyle that did not offend or hurt anyone. His people loved him. He never once bowed during this dark period when many people made some of the idols out of dates in the morning, only to eat them in the evening to satisfy their hunger. Uthman led an exemplary life, never committing any shameful deed or crime. In a time when people consumed alcohol like water, when alcohol flowed through the veins like blood, and when houses were converted into wine cellars, he did not even drink one drop of alcohol. It was as if God was guarding and preparing him for the future. Even during the period of *the Age of Ignorance*, he warned about the dangers of alcohol consumption:

"Alcohol wipes out reason which is the most beautiful blessing that God has bestowed on a human being, so, it befits a human being to use his reason for taking wings and ascending towards the heights of humanity."

How Uthman Remembers Those Days

Uthman speaks about those days this way:

"I shall be hopeful by virtue of ten things when I appear before my Lord:

First: I am the fourteenth of those pioneers who have been honored with Islam.

Second: I used my wealth to equip the Army of Hardships for war.

Third: I compiled the Holy Qur'an in the order that God's Messenger had left.

Fourth: The Messenger of God married me first to one of his daughters and later to another daughter after the former's death.

Fifth: I did not sing the songs nor recite the poems of *the Age of Ignorance*.

Sixth: I did not lie to anyone for any reason and did not cheat anyone in my business.

Seventh: I never touched my private parts with my right hand after I pledged allegiance to and promised the Messenger of God, and this was a promise of great importance.

Eighth: I did not reach any Friday in which I did not set a slave free who was at my disposal.

Ninth: I did not drink even a drop of alcohol during the Age of Ignorance.

Tenth: I never committed adultery, nor even attempted it, neither after entering into the bright atmosphere of Islam nor during the Age of Ignorance."

Uthman lived a life as though he were a Muslim before Islam. It was predestined that he was going to be one of those who would shoulder Islam in the future. As such, God the Almighty did not permit even a small indiscretion to be a source of disgrace for him afterwards.

There are times during which consuming alcohol or amusing one's self with women are regarded as ordinary affairs. The Age of Ignorance was such a time in which every sort of denial and heresy were committed openly and easily. Much effort and zeal are needed in such periods to avoid being dragged into sin. Therefore, Uthman's leading a virtuous life in such a time is significant for the sake of acknowledging his grandeur.

Fondness and Sympathy of the People of Quraysh

The people of Quraysh loved Uthman who stood out as a monument of modesty and civility among them. His social status, wealth, and good temper, in addition to his virtuous character captivated them. This love of the People of Quraysh towards him would manifest itself on the day of

Hudaybiya. Years later, a Quraysh woman composing poems for her child could not help praising him:

> I swear I love you my son,
> Just like the Quraysh loves Uthman.

CHAPTER 2

After He Embraced Islam

A picture of the Ka'ba

AFTER HE EMBRACED ISLAM

Uthman's Conversion to Islam

The story of Uthman's conversion to Islam is inspiring. During the Age of Ignorance, Uthman became extremely sad when he heard that the Prophet had married his daughter, Ruqayya, to Utba, the son of his uncle Abu Lahab. Uthman had wanted to marry Ruqayya very much and had wanted to be the son-in-law of the Messenger of God. Upon hearing the news, he sought the comfort of his aunt Sa'da bint Kariz, a very smart, sagacious, and elderly woman. She was the one who gave him the good news of a Prophet that would end idol worshipping in the future. She also told Uthman that this Prophet will invite humanity to worship

Allah, the one and only God, and that Uthman will accept his invitation.

Years after accepting Islam, Uthman recounted what had happened after his aunt had told him about the coming of a Prophet:

"While I was pondering what my aunt had told me, I met my friend Abu Bakr and shared with him what she had just said to me. Abu Bakr said:

'Uthman, I swear by God that your aunt is telling you the truth. Felicitations! Truth and reality cannot blend with untruth and false near you, as you are a wise and astute person.'

Abu Bakr continued:

'What a pity for our people! They are worshipping idols which are worthless and having no power. They are nothing but tongueless stones, neither seeing nor hearing.'

'Yes, you are right,' I told Abu Bakr.

'What your aunt told you has proven to be true, Uthman. God has sent the long-awaited Messenger who shall be the guide and the source of righteousness for all humanity, bringing the religion of truth and justice.'

'Who is he O Abu Bakr?' I asked.

'He is Muhammad, the son of Abdullah and the grandson of Abdul Muttalib', Abu Bakr replied.

'Is he Muhammad *al-Amin* (the Faithful and the Trustworthy)?" I asked immediately.

'Yes, that is his very self!' said Abu Bakr.

'Will you introduce me to him?' I then asked Abu Bakr.

'Surely, let us go and see him together,' Abu Bakr said, and we both went to the Prophet.

As soon as the Messenger of God saw me, he said:

'O Uthman! Respond favorably to God's message. I am the Messenger sent by God to you in particular and to the whole of humanity in general.'

Upon his words, my heart became full of serenity. I acknowledged his Messengership and voluntarily made the testimony of faith:

'I testify that there is no deity but God, and I testify that Muhammad is God's Messenger.'"

His Marriage with Ruqayya

The Messenger of God married Khadija, the mother of the believers, and they had six children, Qasim, Zaynab, Ruqayya, Umm Kulthum, Fatima, and Abdullah. Upon reaching marriageable age, the Prophet married Zaynab to Abu al-As ibn ur-Rabi, the son of Khadija's aunt. Ruqayya and Umm Kulthum were married to Utba and Utayba, respectively, both of whom were sons of Abu Lahab, the uncle of the Messenger of God. When the Prophet began publically conveying God's message in Mecca, Abu Lahab and some of his family members became increasingly hostile to God's Messenger. And after the revelation of *Tabbat (the Qur'anic chapter which foretells the perishing of Abu Lahab and his wife)* Abu Lahab, his wife Umm Jamil, and other notables of the Quraysh disccused it among themselves and then told Utba and Utayba:

"Divorce the daughters of Muhammad and send them back to their father's home. If you do so, we will marry you to the most beautiful girls in Mecca."

"We will promptly divorce them," replied Utba and Utayba.

Not satisfied with the impact of his decision, Utayba went to Messenger of God and told him:

"O Muhammad! I do not love you and do not accept the religion you say you propagate. I also divorce your daughter. There will no longer be a son-in-law and father-in-law relationship between you and me. I no longer love and respect you, and you also do not love me anymore."

Utayba's words hurt the Prophet very much. In addition to his verbal assault, Utayba lunged at him.

"O my Lord! Scourge him with one of your dogs," prayed the Messenger of God.

Not long after this incident, Utayba went to Damascus to trade. When he and his associates rested at a place named Zarqa, a lion appeared and started roaming around them. Utayba instantly recalled the words of God's Messenger and yelled:

"Oh my God, this lion will dismember me. Ibn Abi Kabsha (implying the Messenger of God) is in Mecca. However, everybody should know that he is my murderer."

After a while, the lion disappeared. However, when everyone was sleeping, it returned and attacked Utayba, dismembering him.

When Uthman heard that Utayba had divorced Ruqayya, he was overjoyed. God's Massenger then married his daughter Ruqayya to Uthman, and Khadija housed them in their home.

The below words echoed in Mecca upon their marriage:

The ever beautiful wife and the finest looking man

Here are Ruqayya and her spouse Uthman

The Messenger of God Gives Fatherly Advice to His Daughter Ruqayya

The Prophet used to visit Ruqayya and Uthman and inquire about their health. In one such visit, he saw Ruqayya pouring water over Uthman's head and helping him to wash his hair. Our Master, peace and blessings be upon him, stated:

"O my dear daughter! Treat Abu Abdullah well and do not sadden him. He is the one who ethically resembles me most among my Companions."

How Uthman Was Tortured and Persecuted because of His Conversion to Islam

Uthman's dignity and tribal pedigree did not shield him from the Quraysh after his conversion to Islam. His uncle Hakam ibn Abu al-As tortured him a lot. One day Hakam ordered some of the family members to catch Uthman and yell at him, as they tied up Uthman's hands and feet:

"Are you abandoning the religion of your ancestors and converting to Muhammad's religion? I will never set you free if you do not change your mind."

Patiently enduring his uncle's tortures, Uthman shouted at him:

"I swear that I will never leave my religion. I will not leave my Prophet and Messenger until the last moment of my life."

No matter how bitterly his uncle tortured him, Uthman stuck to his faith in God and His Messenger. When his uncle realized that Uthman would not change his mind, he let him go. Once Islam settles into a heart, it is impossible to remove it. Love of God and His Messenger were indelibly engraved on the mind and heart of Uthman.

Migration of Uthman and His Wife Ruqayya to Abyssinia

The situation of early Muslims in Mecca was worsening day by day. The believers suffered tortures and persecutions of all kinds. As a precautionary step against such persecutions, the Prophet sent a group of his early Companions, including Uthman and his wife Ruqayya, to Abyssinia where Negus was reigning. There were five women and ten men who made this first journey.

"Uthman and his wife are the first couple who migrated since the time of the Prophet Lot," God's Messenger said.

In Abyssinia, Ruqayya gave birth to a son named Abdullah and Uthman was thus called Abu Abdullah (the father of Abdullah). However, Abdullah died at the age of six.

It was very difficult for those who migrated to Abyssinia to get accurate news from Mecca. One day they were told that the Meccans had stopped torturing and persecuting the believers. Some of those who migrated returned to Mecca, only to discover that the news was not true.

When the Prophet met a woman who had just returned from Abyssinia, he asked her if she saw his daughter and son-in-law.

"Yes, I saw them," the woman replied.

"How were they?" the Prophet continued.

"I saw Uthman helped his wife mount a donkey and led the donkey by pulling its bridle," said the woman.

"May God be helper and friend of both of them. Uthman is the first man who had to migrate with his wife since the time of Prophet Lot," God's Messenger added.

He Was Appointed as the Leader of the Early Migrants to Abyssinia

The Prophet appointed Uthman the leader of the first caravan that migrated to Abyssinia. The wisdom of this decision is easy to understand:

Firts of all, Uthman had a gentle nature and it was difficult for him to endure the atmosphere of persecution in Mecca.

Secondly, he was engaged in trade for years and had led many caravans. Thus, he was an experienced traveler. He also had the finanical means to support the caravan and the others in the group.

Upon their return to Mecca from Abyssinia, Uthman and his wife realized that the situation in Mecca was not as they were told and that Muslims were still being persecuted. When God's Messenger gave permission to migrate to Medina, Uthman left with his wife Ruqayya as soon as he could. In Medina, they were the guest of Aws ibn Thabit, who was the brother of the famous poet Hasan ibn Thabit. Later, when God's Messenger migrated to Medina and made the *Ansar* (the Muslim inhabitants of Medina) and the *Muhajirun* (the Muslim migrants from Mecca to Medina) brothers of each other, he paired Uthman and Aws.

His Life in Medina

The Meccan Muslims who migrated to Medina left all their wealth and properties in Mecca, and thus, they were living under harsh economical conditions in Medina. However, they were blessed with a great reward as the Hijra. The *Muhajirun* received the merits and benefits of the Hijra; the *Ansar*, as helpers to them, received the merits and benefits of safeguarding the *Muhajirun*. This was explained in the Qur'an: "Indeed, those who have believed and emigrated and fought with their wealth and lives in the cause of God and those who gave shelter and aided — they are allies of one another" (Anfal 8:72).

Only two years after the Hijra, the Muslims fought in the Battle of Badr. Every Muslim wanted to participate, as this was the first battle against the polytheists. The Archangel Gabriel told to the Prophet:

"O Muhammad! The angels in the heaven who participated in the battle of Badr are deemed as pioneers among us just as those Companions of you who participated in it are deemed as pioneers among you."

The Battle of Badr

Badr was a small township at approximately 160 km southwest of Medina and 30 km east of the Red Sea coast. Badr was located at a cross section where the Mecca-Medina road intersected with the Syrian caravan road. Its inhabitants were peasants who made their living with the money they had earned from agriculture and from the services they provided to the caravans that stopped there. A third source of income was the annual fair, which lasted eight days.

During the second Hijra year, a large caravan under the leadership of Abu Sufyan headed for Syria. The majority of the notables of Quraysh had goods that they seized from the Meccan Muslims. When the Prophet learned of the caravan, he gathered his Companions and told them to raid it at Badr on its way back to Mecca. The Messenger of God, peace and blessings be upon him, invited all of his Companions from the *Ansar* and the *Muhajirun* to participate, noting that if they were successful, the Meccan polytheists would fall into a deep economic crisis.

Ten days before departing from Medina to Badr, the Prophet charged Talha ibn Ubaydullah and Said ibn Zayd with the duty of gathering information about the caravan. However, they did not return from their mission until the day of the battle. Fortunately, our Master had sent out other scouts as well. He finally departed from Medina by deputizing his *muazzin* Abdullah ibn Ummu Maktum, who was blind, on his behalf. Later, he transferred this deputation to Abu Lubaba.

Meanwhile, as he approached the Hejaz on his way back from Syria, Abu Sufyan learned that the Prophet was preparing to raid the caravan. He immediately dispatched Damdam ibn Amr al-Ghifari to Mecca in order to seek help from the Quraysh. At the same time, in order to prevent the caravan from falling into an ambush, he led the caravan on the coastal route, which was far from Badr and seldomly used. When the Quraysh heard that their caravan was in jeopardy and they risked losing everything, a thousand armed men, gathered from almost all branches of the Quraysh tribe, departed from Mecca under the command of Abu Jahl.

Meanwhile, God's Messenger who had encamped with his army near Badr sent Zubayr ibn al-Awwam, Ali ibn Abi Talib, and Sa'd ibn Abi Waqqas to the water wells of Badr to gather information about the caravan.

At that time, the Prophet and his Companions did not know yet that the Quraysh army had arrived at Badr from Mecca.

Taking into account the number of camels slaughtered each day for food, the Muslims estimated that the Quraysh army was composed of around one thousand men. Ammar ibn Yasir and Abdullah ibn Mas'ud who were sent by the Prophet as scouts returned in the early hours of the morning and reported that a large number of Quraysh people were encamped.

When the Quraysh discovered from their slaves who had returned to the encampment that the Muslims were camped near the water wells of Badr, they were alarmed and began to take measures to prevent a raid.

However, the heavy rain of that night did not let either side move.

The battle started with individual duels and concluded with an absolute Muslim victory by midafternoon. Seventy polytheists were killed, including Abu Jahl who was a fierce enemy of Islam and the Prophet. Seventy others were taken captive.

In return, only fourteen of the Companions were martyred in this battle. The Messenger of God buried them after performing the funeral prayer. He buried the corpses of the Quraysh as well. The Companions of the Prophet were elated when he told them the good news that the sins of the Muslims who participanted at the Battle of Badr were forgiven by God.

Not everybody, however, participated in this battle. Uthman, though he very much had wanted to participate, could not because his wife Ruqayya was ill and our Master asked him to stay back to take care of her. Nevertheless, as per a *hadith* (saying) of the Prophet the nonparticipants who had a legitimate excuse also received the merits of those who participated in the battle. Additionally, our Master reserved Uthman's share of the booty from the battle, considering him among the participants. Wasn't the contentment of God's Messenger also the contentment of God after all?

Our Mother Ruqayya Becoming Ill

Our mother Ruqayya became ill before the Battle of Badr, and Uthman stayed with her as requested by the Messenger of God. When Zayd ibn Haritha brought the news of victory of Badr to Medina, Ruqayya was already dead.

Before she died, Ruqayya was very sad that her husband could not participate at the battle and felt responsible for it. Another cause of sadness for Ruqayya was that her sister Zaynab had stayed in Mecca where believers were heavily persecuted. Zaynab had played both the role of an older sister and as a mother after Khadija had passed away.

In her last breath, Ruqayya's eyes were streaming with tears, her loyal husband Uthman was wiping them and not leaving her side for a moment.

Ruqayya drew her last breath as she recited the *kalimatush shahada* (the testimony of faith). She acknowledged her father's Prophethood with her last breath, although he was not with her. The Prophet was preparing for his *ummah*'s (the global community of Muslim believers) future, for which everything was worth sacrificing.

As Paradise is the ultimate meeting place for the faithful in the Hereafter, what is a temporary separation from our loved ones?

Umm Ayman washed the body of our deceased mother Ruqayya and Uthman performed the funeral prayer. She was buried in the *Jannatul Baqi* Cemetery. Zayd ibn Haritha rushed to the people of Medina on his camel to inform them the good news that God's Messenger was alive and the battle was won.

Upon his return from the Battle of Badr, our Prophet received the news of his daughter's death and grieved over her. He rushed to *Jannatul Baqi*, prayed at her grave, and supplicated God to forgive her sins.

There is a narrative involving our Prophet and his daughter by Abu Hurayra.

One day, the Prophet visited his daughter Ruqayya as he held a comb in his hand. Ruqayya combed her father's blessed hair with that comb.

The Prophet asked her:

"What do you think of Abu Abdullah (Uthman)"?

"He is a nice and good-natured spouse," she replied.

Our Prophet said:

"Uthman is the one who resembles me most among my Companions."

Abdullah ibn Umar, an Egyptian, and Uthman

An Egyptian, who traveled from Egypt to Mecca to perform the *Hajj* (pilgrimage), met with Abdullah ibn Umar. He asked Abdullah ibn Umar:

"O Abdullah! In God's name, please tell me the truth. Did not Uthman participate at the Battle of Badr?"

Abdullah ibn Umar replied:

"No, he did not participate because his wife was sick and the Prophet asked him to stay and take care of her."

Indeed our Prophet said:

"O Uthman! You acquired merit as a *mujahid* (a fighter for Islam) who participated at the Battle of Badr. You deserved as much share from the booty of Badr as a *mujahid* who participated in it."

His Marriage with Umm Kulthum after the Death of Ruqayya

Umm Kulthum is the third daughter of the Prophet. Like her older sister Ruqayya, she was married to one of the sons of Abu Lahab, Utayba. The marriage was broken to insult God's Messenger. Umm Kulthum was then living at her father's house in Mecca with her younger sister Fatima. The two girls assisted their mother in housework. Umm Kulthum was among those whom the Prophet sent to Medina during the Hijra before his own departure from Mecca.

Umm Kulthum's older sister Ruqayya died while she was waiting for their father in Medina after the Battle of Badr.

Even a year later, the sorrow arising from the death of Ruqayya remained. The Quraysh also were mourning the death of their kindred whom they lost at the Battle of Badr, as well as nursing a grudge for taking revenge. Uthman was particularly sad that his son-in-law relationship with God's Messenger had ended with Ruqayya's death.

After Ruqayya died, Umar was contemplating marrying his daughter Hafsa to Uthman, as Hafsa's husband had died. He considered Uthman dependable and virtuous.

Umar asked Uthman if he would marry his daughter Hafsa. Uthman did not give any answer to him right away. Umar then told the Prophet what had happened. The Messenger of God told Umar:

"O Umar! I am proposing you a better thing than this. I will marry Hafsa and Umm Kulthum to Uthman."

The Prophet said to Uthman not long after this:

"O Uthman! Archangel Gabriel told me to marry Umm Kulthum to you. And I am going to marry her to you with the dowry of Ruqayya."

From that point on, Uthman has been referred to as *Dhun-Nurayn* (the Bearer of the Two Pure Lights) due to his marriage with two daughters of the Prophet — the bearer of the first created *nur* (pure light).

The Treaty of Hudaybiya

The *Muhajirun* missed Mecca and their relatives who still lived there. They also missed visiting the Ka'ba. Both Uthman and his wife Umm Kulthum were among the 1400 Companions who set off for *Umra* (the lesser pilgrimage) together with the Prophet six years after the Hijra.

While our Prophet and his Companions were waiting at Hudaybiya, envoys from both the Muslims and the Quraysh polytheists were exchanged. The Prophet first asked Umar to be his envoy. Umar told him:

"O Messenger of God! I am a tough-natured person. I cannot stand by if they say something unfavorable to me. You know the hostility between me and the Quraysh. Reconciliation between us would be difficult. However, if you let me I will advise you of someone. That is Uthman. The Quraysh love Uthman. He is a soft-hearted person and does not get angry quickly like me. Please send him as your special envoy, O Messenger of God!"

Taking Umar's advice, God's Messenger called for Uthman and told him:

"O Uthman! I want you to go to the Quraysh. Tell them that we have not come to fight with them. Our intention is just to make *Umra*. We brought sacrificial animals with us and will return to Medina upon presenting them to God.

Uthman in Mecca as a Special Envoy

Uthman set off alone for Mecca without any hesitation. He was a member of the Quraysh and had many relatives in Mecca. Also, many Meccans knew him well because he had traded for them. He passed the borderline of the *Haram* (the inviolate zone of Ka'ba). When he arrived at the place called Balda, he met with an armed Quraysh detachment. They would have probably harmed him if his relative, Aban ibn Said, had not been with the detachment.

"O people of Quraysh! Do know that I have taken Uthman under my patronage. Whoever lays a finger on him shall find me against him," he said.

Uthman safely arrived at Mecca and conveyed Prophet Muhammad's message to the Meccans. He first invited them to Islam:

"O people of Mecca! Our Prophet is inviting you to Islam. Convert together and be honored with Islam. God will certainly render His religion victorious and His Prophet glorious. Never attempt to touch or harm him."

"You told us what Muhammad asked you to tell us, O Uthman. Now go and tell your friend that what he told you to tell us will never appeal to us," the Meccans replied.

The Meccans did not harm Uthman as they knew him for a long time and he belonged to Banu Umayya, a clan of the Quraysh tribe. They treated him respectfully and told him that he could make *tawaf* (the worship of circumambulating around the Ka'ba):

"O Uthman! You can make *tawaf* alone if you would like to."

They did not hesitate to offer him this as Uthman was under tribal protection. But Uthman rejected the proposal of the Quraysh, stating:

"Making *tawaf* does not interest me unless our Prophet makes it."

However, the false news that Uthman had performed *tawaf* reached some Companions at Hudaybiya who reported it to the Prophet:

"O Messenger of God! You sent Uthman as an envoy to Mecca, but we have heard that Uthman made *tawaf* of the Ka'ba."

Our Prophet responded:

"I do not think that he would make it while we are under such a siege."

"Why not, O Messenger of God! Why shouldn't he make *tawaf* as he was already there?" asked the Companions.

"Uthman cannot make *tawaf* unless we make one," replied our Prophet.

The Prophet's response showed how much he trusted Uthman. His beloved Companions devoted their lives in pursuit of 'us'; the notion of 'me' did not occupy their minds nor their hearts. They could not even imagine thinking in such a way.

The Rumors of Uthman's Assasination

As the Prophet and his Companions waited to hear news from Uthman, they were told that the Meccans had assisinated him. However, this news was also false.

During his stay in Mecca Uthman spread the message of Islam, explaining it to the weak and poor people living there. He conveyed the Prophet's greetings to them and received a favorable response:

"Give our greetings to the Messenger. God who brought His Messenger to Hudaybiya is certainly strong enough to bring him to the heart of Mecca."

After the rumors of Uthman's assassination, the Prophet gathered his Companions and asked them to pledge their loyalty to him and to promise to fight against the polytheists, sacrificing their souls for God's sake if necessary. The Companions did as he requested. Only Jad ibn Qays, a known hypocrite, refused to do so. The first Companion who pledged his loyalty was Abu Sinan. After everyone had finished, the Prophet put one of his hands into his other hand and said:

"This is Uthman's hand."

This homage was called *Bay'atur-Ridhwan* (Oath of Allegiance of God's Pleasure) and was taken under a tree named Samura. Fourteen hundred Companions made the pledge that day.

The same day, a Meccan delegation came to Hudaybiya. There the Quraysh agreed a 10-year truce and the Treaty of Hudaybiya was concluded. Under this treaty, the Prophet and his Companions could make the minor pilgrimage the following year.

The Battle of Tabuk

The Battle of Tabuk is one of the battles that God's Messenger participated in his lifetime. It was rumored that the Byzantine Emperor Heraclius was approaching with a great army towards Medina. The news alarmed the Muslims, but made the neighbouring hostile Arab tribes happy and hopeful.

Although the Prophet normally would secretly organize and launch his expeditions, this time he openly announced his plans, sending envoys to the neighbouring tribes to ask them to provide warriors and munitions.

The people in Medina were suffering from hard times. The weather was very hot. Aridity and famine were wreaking havoc on the community. Furthermore, the much needed dates were due to be harvested soon. But the Messenger of God had already declared mobilization and had started war preparations. Most Muslims were racing against each other to participate in the expedition of Tabuk, which is located on the northwest coast of the Arabian Peninsula. As expected, Uthman was among the volunteers. Many Muslims who came to the Messenger of God excited to participate in the battle left him crying like children because there were not enough camels for them to ride. The Qur'an monumentalized this attitude of them as an exemplary motion: "Nor (can there be any way to blame) those who, when they came to you to provide them with mounts, and you said, 'I cannot find anything whereon to mount you,' they returned, their eyes overflowing with tears for sorrow that they could not find anything to spend (to prepare themselves for the campaign)". (Tawba 9:92).

The Muslim army also did not have sufficient arms and munitions. Upon encouragement of the Messenger of God, Uthman donated hundreds of camels fully equipped. The Messenger of God said:

"I swear to God, whatever Uthman does from now on will not harm him."

The Muslim army was known as the Army of Hardships (*Jayshul Usra*). Uthman's name became prominent in Tabuk because of his generosity. The camels which went to Tabuk in this expedition saluted Uthman in their breathing; the warriors saluted him each time they drank water; the camels and sheep saluted Uthman while being slaughtered.

Some of the Companions described this event:

Abdur Rahman ibn Habbab narrates:

"I witnessed Uthman ibn Affan stand up and say when Messenger of God asked for help to equip the the Army of Hardships:

'O Messenger of God! I donate a hundred camels with their saddles and clothes for God's sake.'

Messenger of God once again encouraged those present to donate to the army. Uthman again stood up and said:

'O Messenger of God! I donate two hundred camels with their saddles and clothes for God's sake.'

Then again the Messenger of God encouraged those present to donate to the army. Uthman stood up again and said:

'O Messenger of God! I donate three hundred camels with their saddles and clothes for God's sake.'"

Abdur Rahman finished his words:

"I saw the Messenger of God step down from the pulpit and say:

'After this donation, no bad deed of Uthman will affect him.'"

Indeed, a man with such behavior would not be expected to act badly.

The Spiritual Rank of Uthman

One day, our mother Umm Kulthum came to the Prophet and asked:

"O Messenger of God! Is my or Fatima's husband more benevolent?"

Our Master kept silent for a while and then said:

"Your husband loves God and His Messenger. God and His Messenger also love your husband."

As our mother Umm Kulthum started to leave, the Messenger of God called her back and said:

"Paradise was shown to me. I did not see anyone among my Companions who had a higher rank than your husband."

Passing of Our Mother Umm Kulthum

Our mother Umm Kulthum passed away in the month of *Sha'aban* (the eighth month of the Islamic calendar), during the ninth year of the Hijra in Medina and in the company of her husband. The destiny of the Prophet's daughter was being revealed in the consecutive deaths of Zainab, Ruqayya, and Umm Kulthum. Umm Kulthum was buried near her elder sisters. The Messenger of God was very sad. He took a handful of soil and scattered it over her grave while reciting the Qur'anic verse, "From it (earth) We create you, and into it are We returning you, and out of it will We bring you forth a second time" (Ta Ha 20:55).

He also prayed:

"Bismillah, fi sabilillah, ala millat-i Rasulillah" (i.e., in the name of God, in the way of God and in the religion of the Messenger of God").

Uthman was very sad upon the death of his second wife Umm Kulthum. The Prophet said to him in consolation:

"If I had forty daughters, I would have married them all to Uthman."

In another narration, the Messenger of God said:

"Not me, but God has been marrying my daughters to Uthman."

Passing of Uthman's Son Abdullah

Uthman and our mother Ruqayya had a son named Abdullah. Abdullah passed away at the age of six in the month of *Jumada al-awwal* (the fifth month of the Islamic calendar) during the fourth year of the Hijra. He was Uthman's last familial tie to the Prophet. Our Master personally performed little Abdullah's funeral prayer, and Uthman stepped down into the grave and laid his son Abdullah to rest with his own hands.

Rumah Water Well and Uthman's Endowment of It

Another deed of Uthman which exemplifies his generosity was his purchase and endowment of the water well Rumah near Medina. As mentioned in Islamic historical sources, when the Prophet migrated to Medina, only the Rumah water well provided high quality potable water. One narration states that this water well was owned by a Jew belonging to the Banu Ghifar tribe and the water was sold at a price as high as one silver *dirham* per *qirba* (leather bottle) [a chicken cost one *dirham* then]. The well did not have much water, however. Considering the need for water, God's Messenger wanted some-one to purchase the well and to dig it deeper in order to increase the water and distribute it for free. He said:

"Whoever buys, rehabilitates, and puts the Rumah water well into service of the people, for him is Paradise in return of this good deed."

Uthman, upon this promise, purchased this water well by paying 35,000 *dirhams* and then put it into service of all human beings.

Uthman's generosity is a subject worthy of discussion. We shall return to this subject with more examples in the pages ahead.

The Expansion Works of the Prophet's Mosque

After completion of the Prophet's Mosque (*Masjid an-Nabawi*), the Companions of the Prophet, whether they lived a short or long distance from it, performed their prayers in the Prophet's Mosque with the Messenger of God five times a day. They listened to his sermons and *talks*. The Messenger of God conveyed to them God's commands and prohibitions and gave them advice. In the Prophet's Mosque, they were learning everything pertaining to Islam and religious life.

The Prophet's Mosque also was a place for mustering expeditions and for meeting when returning from expeditions.

The Prophet's Mosque eventually became too small for all of the Companions to gather. God's Messenger proposed purchasing the land adjacent to the Prophet's Mosque to enlarge the space. He said:

"Which one of you would like to acquire this land, annex it to the Prophet's Mosque, and so prepare a better place for himself in Paradise?"

An imaginary picture of the Prophet's Mosque (Masjid an-Nabawi) of the early period.

Uthman, in order to benefit from this promise, bought the land for 25,000 *dirhams* and immediately donated it to the Prophet's Mosque.

Uthman in the Eye of the Prophet

Our mother Aisha narrates:

"One day, Abu Bakr came and sought permission to visit the Messenger of God. At that time, our Master was lying in his bed and my quilt was on him. The Messenger of God let Abu Bakr in without changing his own position. They talked and when their discussion was over, Abu Bakr left. After some time, Umar came and sought permission to visit the Messenger of God. Our Master also let Umar in without changing his own position. Some time after Umar's departure, Uthman sought permission to visit the Messenger of God. This time, the Messenger of God got up, sat on his bed, tidied himself up, and said to me:

'Tidy up your clothes.'

After that, he let Uthman in. And after serving his purpose, Uthman too departed.

Upon Uthman's departure, I asked him:

'O Messenger of God! While you stood idly by when Abu Bakr and Umar came, you made yourself presentable upon Uthman's visit. What is the reason for this difference?'

'Uthman is a very modest person. If I would have let him in while I was in my previous position and without tidying myself, I was afraid he would have left without sharing his thoughts with me,' God's Messenger replied."

Uthman and Promise of Paradise

In a narrative by Abu Musa al-Ash'ari, in which he said:

"I walked together with God's Messenger. He entered into a garden belonging to someone from the *Ansar* and told me after completing his own purpose there:

'O Abu Musa! Watch the door well. Don't let anyone in without my prior permission.'

Then, someone came and knocked the door.

'Who is it?', I asked.

'Abu Bakr', the man said.

'O Messenger of God! Abu Bakr is here and is seeking permission to enter', I said.

'Open the door for him and give him the promise of Paradise', the Messenger of God said.

I opened the door, Abu Bakr came in and I promised him with Paradise.

Then, someone else came and knocked on the door.

'Who is it?', I asked.

'Umar', the man said.

'O Messenger of God! Umar is here and is seeking permission to enter', I said.

'Open the door for him and give him the promise of Paradise', the Messenger of God said.

I opened the door, Umar came in and I promised him with Paradise.

Then, some other person arrived and knocked the door.

'Who is it?', I asked.

'Uthman', the man said.

'O Messenger of God! Uthman is here and is seeking permission to enter', I said.

'Open the door for him and give him the promise of Paradise in exchange for a calamity which he will suffer', the Messenger of God said."

His Grief and Sadness upon the Prophet's Demise

Upon the demise of our Prophet, Uthman, as the other Companions, was distraught.

He remembers those days as follows:

"People began talking among themselves while I was sitting on the roof of my house. I then heard that people had sworn their allegiance to Abu Bakr. According to what I later came to know, Umar passed by my house and saluted me. But I did not hear his salutation, as I was in a deep sadness. Umar went to Caliph Abu Bakr and complained him about me:

'O Abu Bakr! I am so disappointed. I saluted Uthman while I was passing by his home, but he did not respond to my salutation.'"

The Famine During the Caliphate of Abu Bakr

A serious famine arose in Medina during the Caliphate of Abu Bakr. During that time, a caravan belonging to Uthman was returning from Damascus. As in Mecca, Uthman made his living by export-import trading and was successful in his business. This particular caravan had one thousand camels and was loaded with cereals and foodstuffs. When they heard about the caravan's arrival, the Companions rushed to Uthman and said:

"O Uthman! We have come to know that a caravan of a thousand camels all loaded with cereals, and foodstuffs have reached you. As you know, there is a famine in Medina. Sell the goods to us, so that we both satisfy our needs and distribute the rest to the needy people in Medina. They started bargaining with Uthman to buy the goods, but he would not agree to sell it to them. He told them:

"There is someone else who is ready to pay more than you for this cargo, thus I will sell all of it to that one who is paying more than you."

The Companions became annoyed with his attitude. They rushed to the newly elected Caliph Abu Bakr and complained to him about Uthman:

"O Commander of the Faithful! Uthman's caravan has arrived from Damascus. We proposed him such a price for a scale of wheat. But he would not sell it to us and said that there is someone else paying him more than us. Is it fair for him to treat us like this in a time of famine?"

Abu Bakr said to them:

"Don't think of him unfavorably. He has been honored with being the son-in-law of the Messenger of God and also of being his friend in Paradise. Presumably, there is some sort of misunderstanding. Let's go to him together and try to find out from him what is going on."

They went to Uthman.

"O Uthman! These friends are very upset that you would not sell your merchandise to them. Why would you not do so?" asked Abu Bakr.

"O Caliph of the Messenger of God! Yes, that is true. They gave seven to one for my merchandise. But I sold my merchandise to someone else who is paying much more! God the Almighty is giving seven hundred to one! Thus, I sold my merchandise to Him!" replied Uthman.

Uthman freely distributed all his merchandise that arrived with the caravan to the poor of Medina with the hope of attaining the pleasure of God. He also sacrificed all of the camels in the caravan and distributed the meat to the poor and needy.

With his deed, Uthman brought abundance and prosperity to Medina. Abu Bakr was very happy with Uthman's generosity and he kissed Uthman on the forehead.

That night, Abdullah ibn Abbas saw the Messenger of God in his dream.

Abdullah ibn Abbas recounts:

"The Messenger of God was wearing clothes and footwear made out of *nur* (pure light) and holding in his hand a bunch of *nur*. I told him:

'O Messenger of God! I miss you and your voice very much. Why are you moving so fast?', our Master told me in my dream:

'O Ibn Abbas! Uthman gave such alms that God accepted his alms and rewarded him with a heavenly wedding. We are invited to his wedding in Paradise.'"

His Proposal of Keeping Records

After Muslim lands expanded due to territorial gains by conquests, Caliph Umar established a consultative committee composed of many of the leading Companions. He asked them how to manage and keep records of the ever growing financial system.

Uthman suggested:

"O Commander of the Faithful! People have become very rich. Problems will arise after a short while because people are not keeping records of their exchanges of goods among themselves. We should develop a public recording system."

Umar found this proposal acceptable, so he established the *diwans* (public records office) and all monetary and commodity exchanges began to be registered.

Umar's Death and the Foretoken of Uthman's Caliphate

Abu-Lu'lu'a, the Zoroastrian slave of Mughira ibn Shu'ba, came to Umar one day and complained about his master. The slave told Umar that he had an agreement with his master, but his master was demanding a tax higher than that of their agreement. Having extensive experience in the particularities and intricacies of administration and administratorship, Caliph Umar asked him to explain what had happened in more detail. After listening to the slave, Umar adjudged that what his master asked from him was not too much. Umar had heard that the slave Abu Lu'lu'a was a skilful grain mill maker. He thus gave him an order to make a grain mill for himself as well. A few days later, Caliph Umar was leading the congregation for the Dawn Prayer in the Prophet's Mosque. Abu Lu'lu'a snuck through the congregation and stabbed Umar with his dagger from behind,

killing him. Umar's blessed body was bleeding.
Even in this circumstance, the first thing Umar
said was that Abdur Rahman ibn Awf should
lead the congregation and complete the prayer.
Umar praised God when he learned that the
person who had stabbed him was a Zoroastrian.
He said that it would have been much worse if
a Muslim who was angry with him committed
such an act. Umar thought that he was going
to die and did not want the Muslims to be left
without a Caliph. He thus nominated six persons, all of whom were among the ten who had
been promised Paradise: Uthman ibn Affan, Ali
ibn Abi Talib, Talha ibn Ubaydillah, Zubayr ibn
al-Awwam, Sa'd ibn Abi Waqqas, and Abdur
Rahman ibn Awf. If his beloved Abu Ubayda ibn
al-Jarrah would have been alive, Umar probably
would have elected him as Caliph. The Prophet
had said about him: "Abu Ubayda is the trustee
of this *ummah*".

CHAPTER 3

His Caliphate

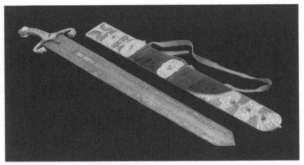

Sword of Uthman ibn Affan
Topkapi Palace Museum, Inventory number 2/3775

HIS CALIPHATE

His Election as Caliph

At the 24th year of the Hijra, on the third day of the month of *Muharram* (the first month of the Islamic calendar), Uthman accepted allegiance from the Companions. That year was called the Year of *Ruaf* (Year of Showers) because it rained heavily in and around Medina. However, it was not clear whether the sky was delighted with Uthman's Caliphate or sad for the unhappy incidents Uthman would incur in the future. The *Ahlush Shura* (The People of Consultation) had gathered around Uthman on the day the people made allegiance to him. He went to the Prophet's Mosque before the afternoon prayer and delivered a speech. Suhayb, who was then the *muazzin* (caller to prayer) of the Prophet's Mosque, recited the *adhan* (call to prayer). The Madinans gathered in the Prophet's Mosque and between *adhan* and *iqama* (call to prayer immediately before the prayer begins), submitted their allegiance to Uthman in groups of a hundred. Something which did not happen during the periods of the previous Caliphs happened that day. Muslims arrived from other cities in delegations to submit their allegiances to him. When he climbed the pulpit to address the congregation, Uthman was likely the most worried and sorrowful of those who were present. He never desired administratorship. His facial expression reflected his concern over the heavy burden of such a responsibility. He gave advice in his sermon. The people's allegiance continued afterwards.

In one of the *hadith* narrated by Aysha, she conveyed the following statement of the Prophet:

"O Uthman! One day God will attire you a shirt. Do not take it off for their sake if they ask you to take it off."

This shirt was indeed the shirt of the Caliphate. A Prophetic report of our Master from the realm of the unseen became visible after years.

What He Said in His First Sermon

Uthman delivered a sermon to the people when they gathered in the Prophet's Mosque. In this sermon he said:

> I accepted and assumed a heavy burden of responsibility. I am a person who follows his predecessors, not an innovator or superstitious. I abide by God's Book, the Qur'an, and the practice of His Prophet. You have been enjoying the blessings of peace and security provided to you by Islam. You have come closer with these blessings in the twilight of your lives. I wish that your lives end with gratitude. You strive your best, day and night. Know very well that the world is deceitful in its essence. Do not let the mundane life deceive you. Do not put on grand airs before God and take your lesson from those who became illuminated. Do not have a devil-may-care attitude like the heedless, but be wakeful. God is certainly not inattentive to what you have been doing. Where are they now? Where are those who once loved and were much occupied with affairs of the world? Those who were once men of means? Those who once constructed palaces and caravanserais? Where are those mundane dynasties that reigned for a long time and lived in luxury and extravagancy? Hasn't the world

*betrayed them? Take a lesson from them and
do not overestimate this worthless world which
is held in contempt by God. Make preparations
for the Hereafter which is your eternal residence.*

Uthman said that the Qur'anic verse from
the chapter Kahf exemplifies this fact and concluded his sermon by reciting it:

*And strike to them a parable of the present,
worldly life: (it is) like water that We send
down from the sky, and the vegetation of the
earth mingles with it (flourishing abundantly).
Then it turns into dry stubble which the winds
scatter about. God is absolutely able to do all
things. (Kahf 18:45)*

His First Action

Uthman made this move at the recommendation of the previous Caliph Umar. He also explained it to ease Mughira's heart:

"I have replaced Mughira with Sa'd not because of any mistake or any treason of him, but
at the recommendation of the Caliph before me."

Sa'd ibn Abi Waqqas was the first governor appointed during the Caliphate of Uthman. Before
the Caliphate of Uthman, Sa'd already had served
as the governor of Kufa for a year or so.

Uthman led the other pilgrims on the *Hajj* during his first year as Caliph. The Companions of the Prophet regarded changes in leadership as emancipation, because responsibility of any mission was very burdensome.

The Restoration of the Ka'ba

During the 26th year of the Hijra, Uthman ordered that the Ka'ba be restored. He also ordered the expansion of the Prophet's Mosque by legal expropriation of some of the houses next to the Prophet's Mosque. He reimbursed some of the owners of the houses. With other owners, he deposited the money in the *Baytul Mal* (the House of Wealth) because they did not want to sell their properties. He later demolished their houses. When they complained to Uthman, he imprisoned them, stating:

"If Umar would have treated you in such a way, you would not have complained to him."

Khalid ibn Asid intervened and asked Uthman for their forgiveness and he set them free.

Appointment of Abdullah ibn Sa'd as Governor of Egypt

In the same year, Amr ibn al-As was removed from the post of *Sahib al-Kharaj* (the Revenue

Collector) of Egypt and Uthman's foster brother, Abdullah ibn Sa'd ibn Abi Sarh, was nominated to replace him. Subsequently, disputes arose between them. Abdullah ibn Sa'd wrote a letter to Uthman, telling him that Amr was interfering in Egypt's financial affairs. Amr also wrote a letter to Uthman and reported that Abdullah was interfering in military affairs. Uthman told Amr to return to Medina and removed him from his post administering the financial affairs. He then appointed Abdullah ibn Sa'd in Amr's place. Now, Abdullah ibn Sa'd was responsible for both Egypt's financial and military affairs.

Abdullah ibn Sa'd was one of the commanders of Egypt and Uthman ordered him to conquer other lands in Africa. Uthman told him:

"If you succeed in your conquests, I will give you the one-fifth of one-fifth of the booties seized during those conquests."

Abdullah ibn Sa'd reminded Caliph Uthman about his promise and asked Uthman for military support, along with new conscripts. Uthman, after consultation with notables of the Companions, decided to move forward with the conquest of Africa and equipped a brigade from Medina and despatched them to Egypt under the command of

Abdullah ibn Sa'd. When this Madinan brigade arrived, he joined them to his army and they began their conquest of the Africa interior.

Much later, Uthman sent Abdullah ibn Zubayr and soldiers under his command from Medina to North Africa to bring back the news of the Muslims' conquest of Africa. By traveling quickly, Abdullah ibn Zubayr and his soldiers were able to meet up with Abdullah ibn Sa'd and his army. When they arrived, Abdullah ibn Sa'd and his army were happy for their support and showed their happiness by reciting *takbir* (proclaiming the greatness of God).

After the African conquests, Abdullah ibn Sa'd returned to Egypt. This military expedition lasted about a year and three months. Only three Muslims were martyred during the battles. One-fifth of the booty seized during this expedition was sent to Medina. When the war booties arrived from Africa, Marwan ibn al-Hakam asked to purchase them for five hundred thousand *dinar*s, to which Uthman agreed.

Expedition to Andalusia

Uthman ordered Abdulllah ibn Nafi ibn Husayn and Abdullah ibn Nafi ibn Qays to arrange a military campaign to Andalusia after Tunisia and North Africa were conquered. The two commanders traveled to Andalusia by sea. Uthman had written to them and the people:

"I say to you after *bismillah* (in the name of God) and *alhamdulillah* (praise to God) that Constantinople (Istanbul) will be conquered from the direction of Andalusia."

Conquest of Cyprus Island

After Uthman became Caliph, Muawiya ibn Abu Sufyan wrote him many letters and sought his permission to conduct naval expeditions. Uthman finally gave him permission, even though maritime operations were something that the Muslims had never undertaken. Uthman told Muawiya:

"Do not draft Muslims for this naval operation. Also, do not draw lots from among them either. Leave them alone. Enroll only those who volunteer and equip them with the necessary military supplies."

Muawiya appointed Abdullah ibn Qays, who had an agreement with Bani Fazara tribe, as commander of this naval expedition. Afterwards, the Muslims set sail from Damascus to Cyprus.

Meanwhile, the army which Abdullah ibn Sa'd sent from Egypt arrived and joined them. Muslims conquered Cyprus and the Cypriots agreed to pay the *jizya* (poll tax) of seven thousand *dinars* per year.

The Cypriots paid the same amount of tax to the Byzantium Empire as well. Muslims stopped them from doing so. Additionally, the Cypriots agreed to let the Muslims move their armies through Cyprus to Byzantine lands.

During this expedition to Cyprus, Umm Haram bint Milhan, a foster-aunt of the Prophet died on Cyprus soil. She fell off her horse and broke her neck. This incident verified a saying and a miracle of the Prophet. One day, the Messenger of God visited his foster-aunt Umm Haram at her house in Medina and rested there for a while. He woke up smiling.

"Why have you smiled, O Messenger of God?" asked Umm Haram.

"I saw in my dream that some people from my *ummah* who were fighting for God's sake were sailing on a green sea. It was as if they were sultans ensconced on thrones," our Master replied.

"O Messenger of God! Pray God for me and ask Him to render me one of them as well," said Umm Haram.

"O God! Render her one of them as well," prayed the Messenger of God and he lay back down on the bed. He woke up again smiling after a short while and spoke as before. This time, God's Messenger said:

"Your are among the pioneers not among the last."

Anas ibn Malik remembers those days as follows:

"Umm Haram bint Milhan married with Ubayda ibnus-Samit and they both participated in the naval expedition to Cyprus. It was the time of the Caliphate of Uthman. They went ashore and started walking to Cyprus. The horse she rode suddenly estrapaded, she fell off, and died a martyr."

This was the realization of the Prophetic miracle.

Territorial Borders of the State during His Caliphate

Within less than five years following Uthman's election as Caliph, the Muslims conquered the entire region of North Africa. Marching eastward and northeastward, Muslim armies passed beyond the Caspian Sea, conquering first Tabaristan (Tapuria; former historic regions of southern coasts of the Caspian Sea, known today as Golestan, Mazandaran, and Semnan in Iran) and later *Ma Wara'un-Nahr* (Transoxiana, the ancient name used for the portion of Central Asia corresponding approximately with modern-day Uzbekistan, Tajikistan, and southwest Kazakhstan) and extended the eastern borders of the Islamic state to the Great Wall in China.

Dropping of the Stamp of Messenger of God into the Aris Well

All three of the Prophet Muhammad's Caliphs, Abu Bakr, Umar, and Uthman, used the stamp that he used for state affairs. One day, however, Uthman dropped the stamp into a well named Aris near Medina.

This well had been dug to meet the water needs of the Muslims, but it did not contain much water.

Uthman was sitting beside the well and holding the stamp. The stamp suddenly slipped out of his hand and dropped into the well. Although the well was thoroughly searched and even emptied, the stamp could not found. Uthman promised a large reward to the person who found it, but no one did. Uthman was extremely sad about its loss. When he lost all hope in finding it, he had a similar stamp made, which he wore as a ring until he died.

The original stamp had been made when the Prophet was sending letters to other tribes, states, and nations for the purpose of inviting them to Islam and to God's cause.

Some of his Companions had told him that if his letters were unstamped, they would be ignored. Listening to their advice, the Messenger of God ordered a stamp to be made out of iron and he wore it as a ring. However, the Archangel Gabriel prevented him from using it.

God's Messenger ordered another stamp made, but this time to be made out of copper and he wore it as a ring. Once again Archangel Gabriel told him not to use it.

Our master then ordered a third stamp to be made out of silver and again he wore this stamp as a ring.

This time the Archangel Gabriel told him that he could use it. The stamp made of silver had three lines of wording carved into it. The first line read "Muhammad"; the second "Rasul" (Messenger) and the third line "Allah". He had used this stamp until his death. Abu Bakr also used this stamp until his death. The stamp then passed to Umar after Abu Bakr and then to Uthman after Umar. Uthman used it for a period of six years.

Compilation and Duplication of the Holy Qur'an

The ever-increasing Islamic conquests resulted in affluence and material well-being for the overall Muslim community. Arab Muslims were migrating to new and different cities and regions of the newly conquered lands. The new converts to Islam came from different faiths, cultural backgrounds, and environments; they were in the urgent need of learning their new faith, Islam, and its book, the Holy Qur'an. With exposure to new faiths and cultures, Muslim communities were becoming increasingly alienated with each passing day from the atmosphere of revelation that was intensely experienced during the time of the

Prophet. In every city and town in these newly conquered lands, the new converts were learning and reciting the Holy Qur'an, according to the *qira'at* (methods of recitation) of the particular Companions who had settled and became well-known in those places. For example, in Damascus the Holy Qur'an was being recited according to the *qira'at* of Ubay ibn Ka'b; in Kufa, it was being recited according to the *qira'at* of Abdullah ibn Mas'ud; and in Basra according to the *qira'at* of Abu Musa al-Ash'ari. These Companions also were performing in their regions the Islamic duty of *amr-bil-ma'ruf wa nahy-an-il-munkar* (enjoining what is good and forbiding what is evil) and serving as teachers and guides for people. This separate but simultaneous teaching and learning began to cause controversies among Muslims living in different cities and regions. The newly converted Muslims were naturally not familiar with such things as the seven *ahruf* (the seven dialects) in reading and reciting the Qur'an. Hence, they became confused and suspicious about the differences among the Companions who taught how to recite the Qur'an to the new converts. Although their way of reciting certain words was different, the spelling and thus meaning of words were the same.

Furthermore, absence of the Messenger of God, whose very existence prevented any lasting controversy among the Muslims, exascerbated the disintegration process to the extent that it eventually caused upheavals among Muslims in the various regions.

During the early years of Islam, controversies arose because Muslims belonged to various Arab tribes other than Quraysh, and they read the Qur'an in seven *ahruf* until they became familiar with the Quraysh dialect. Likewise and for similar reasons, in the beginning of Uthman's Caliphate the newly converted non-Arab Muslims also experienced difficulties in correctly reading the Qur'an. One Qur'an teacher taught the *qira'at* of a particular imam, another teacher taught the *qira'at* of another imam. Differences of opinion arose when students of these teachers came together and their teachers then accused each other when they learned of the differences.

The final straw came when the Iraqi and Syrian soldiers who participated at the battles in Armenia and Azerbaijan argued over the reading of the Qur'an. The time had long come for the duplication and distribution of the master copy of the *Mushaf* (the manuscript bound between two boards) in accordance with the way it was written, compiled, and memorized during the age of bliss and tranquility in which the Messenger of God lived and the way it was bound as a book between two boards during the time of Abu Bakr's Caliphate – efforts specifically intended to prevent differences in the reading and recitation of the Qur'an.

In an event narrated in *Sahih al-Bukhari*, Hudhayfa ibn al-Yamani, the commander of the army that participated at the battles in Armenia and Azarbaijan, was terrified when he saw the controversies between the Iraqi and the Syrian soldiers arising over the reading of the Qur'an. Upon returning to Medina from the battle, he immediately found Uthman, even before stopping by his own house, and told him:

"O Commander of the Faithful! Come to the rescue of this *ummah* before they fall into a dispute over the Qur'an, as had the People of the Book (Christians and Jews) once fell into dispute over their Books."

When Uthman heard this, he sent a message to our mother, Hafsa, asking her to send him the master copy of the *Mus'haf* (codex) which had been compiled and entrusted to her by Abu Bakr. Uthman also told her that they would duplicate the *Mus'haf* and give back the original to her.

Hafsa sent him the *Mus'haf* that was in her possession.

For the task of copying the *Mus'haf*, Uthman assigned Abdullah ibn Zubayr, Said ibn al-As, and Abdur Rahman ibn Harith ibn Hisham under the leadership of Zayd ibn Thabit. He instructed them:

"In case you fall into any dispute with Zayd ibn Thabit over the Qur'an, write it in accordance with the Quraysh dialect, as it was revealed in that dialect."

The master copy of the Qur'an that was entrusted to Hafsa was referred to as the *Imam Mus'haf*.

This committee assigned to copy the Qur'an followed Uthman's intructions precisely. Uthman returned the *Imam Mus'haf* to Hafsa and sent the various copies to several Islamic centers. He also ordered the burning of all of the other versions and pages of the Qur'an and private *mus'hafs*.

The actual number of these copies is a matter of dispute. It has been widely accepted that at least four, and at the most eight, exist. One of the copies was kept in Medina, the capital city of the Caliphate, while other copies were sent to such prominent Islamic centers as Kufa, Basra, Damascus, Mecca, Egypt, Yemen, and Bahrain. It should also be noted that Uthman did not make or implement the decision of burning the different versions by himself. In fact, he made this important decision only after consulting with and receiving support from leading Companions. Ali's words below against those who criticized Uthman's decision are illustrative:

"O people! Beware of God and refrain from rushing into extremes about Uthman and saying that he is the burner of the *mus'hafs*. By God, he certainly did this with the consent of the Companions of the Prophet."

Ali later added that if he were Uthman, he too would have done the same thing.

His Expansion and Restoration of the Prophet's Mosque

The Prophet's Mosque had become insufficient for congregations due to the increase of Madina's population during Uthman's Caliphate. The Mosque has not been expanded since the time of the Prophet because the Companions tried to keep it in its original form. Uthman expropriated the houses neighbouring the Prophet's Mosque in order to expand it. This was the first expropriation in the history of Islam. Carved stones were used on the walls of the Mosque and its columns were strenghtened by the use of cast lead. The *minbar* (pulpit) and the *mihrab* (niche in the wall of a mosque) remained as they were during the time of the Messenger of God. However, Uthman added a second minbar, which remains in the Prophet's Mosque to this day and is known as Uthman's minbar.

Uthman's Care for the Needy

Uthman ibn Hunayf narrates: There was a man who from time to time used to visit Uthman. However, Uthman did not pay attention to or care for this man. He presumably was not convinced that he was needy.

This man met Uthman ibn Hunayf and complained to him about Uthman as Caliph.

Uthman ibn Hunayf told him:

"Go and get a kettle full of water, make an ablution (do ritual cleansing), go to the Prophet's Mosque, make two *rak'ats* (units) of prayer, and then pray to God like this: 'O God! I am turning towards You and begging Your help by the mediation of Your Prophet of Mercy. O Prophet Muhammad! I am turning towards my Lord God, the Almighty, by your mediation so that He satisfies my need'. Mention your needs whatever they are after this pray. Then come to me and we will go together to see Uthman."

The two then left each other. The needy man did what Uthman ibn Hunayf told him to do and went to visit Caliph Uthman. He told the man to sit down near him and asked him about his needs. The Caliph was satisfied that he was needy and said:

"I have just now remembered that you have been telling me your needs. For whatever needs you have, come to me from now on."

After having departed, the man met Uthman ibn Hunayf on the road and told him:

"May God reward you. The Caliph did not pay attention to nor satisfy my needs until you spoke to him about me."

Uthman ibn Hunayf told him:

"By God! I have not told Uthman anything about you. But I witnessed such an event before the Messenger of God. A blind man came to the Messenger of God and complained to him about his needs.

'Don't you bear with the circumstance that you are in?', the Messenger of God asked him.

'O Messenger of God! There is no one to help me. My blindness is deeply hurting me', replied the blind man.

'Go and make an ablution. Then make two *raka'ats* of prayer and pray 'O God! I am turning towards You and begging Your help by the mediation of Your Prophet of Mercy. O Prophet Muhammad! I am turning towards my Lord, God the Almighty, by your mediation so that He satisfies my need'. Then, mention your needs whatever they are after this pray,' our Prophet told him.

Then the blind man left us. We remained in the Prophet's Mosque as our conversation lasted long. The blind man returned to the Mosque shortly thereafter and he was no longer blind."

His Advice to Pay Attention to One's Future Wife's Parents

When Abdullah ibn Zubayr returned from the conquest of Ifriqiya (coastal regions of what are today western Libya, Tunisia, and eastern Algeria), Caliph Uthman welcomed him and asked him to stand on the pulpit and tell the congregation about his victory. After Abdullah ibn Zubayr recounted the events of the conquest, Uthman began to speak:

"O Muslims! When marrying your children, evaluate their future spouses with their parents and siblings. I have not seen among Abu Bakr's children or grandchildren anyone who resembles him more than this Abdullah."

Abdullah ibn Zubayr was the son of Asma, the daughter of Abu Bakr. Uthman meant by these words that Abdullah was a courageous and eloquent person like his grandfather, Abu Bakr.

He Invites Hasan to His Wedding

At the time Uthman was getting married, he invited his beloved Hasan ibn Ali ibn Abi Talib to his wedding. Hasan stood by without touching the wedding feast while the other invitees were eating. This attracted Uthman's attention:

"Why are you not eating anything from the wedding feast? Is there anything wrong?" Uthman asked him.

"If I knew that you were going to invite me to your feast, I woul not have made the intention to fast. I am fasting today," replied Hasan.

When he heard Hasan's reply, Uthman ordered that kohl and fine perfumes be brought to Hasan.

"We know how to entertain one who is fasting," Uthman said as he handed Hasan the kohl and fine perfumes.

Uthman's Conversion of Coastal Town Jeddah to a Port

It was the sixth year of the Hijra and Uthman made the decision of transforming the coastal town of Jeddah into a port, instead of the Sha'biya, a port town for Mecca during the Age of Ignorance. Uthman traveled to Jeddah and personally participated in the transformation project. This new port opened up a new route for both merchants and pilgrims, heading to Mecca by sea.

Today, Jeddah is still serving as a port city and is an excellent example for Uthman's vision of urbanization.

Uthman's Leaving the Seller on Approbation

Uthman bought a piece of land from someone. Later he met with the seller and asked him:

"Why are you not delivering the land that you sold to me?"

"You cheated me. Whoever I ask tells me that I am the one who was cheated in this deal," replied the man.

"Is this why you are blaming me? Then select between the money I paid you and your piece of land. You are free to choose either of them," Uthman replied and then narrated the following *hadith* that he had heard from the Prophet:

"May God reward with His paradise the person who behaves soft when buying or selling something, when paying a debt or asking for its payment."

Uthman's Tears

Uthman was a tenderhearted and tearful person. Whenever he stopped by a graveyard, he would begin to cry, so much so that his tears wet his blessed beard.

The people who did not know the reason for his crying asked him:

"O Uthman! You don't cry even when you speak about Paradise and Hell. But you cry whenever you visit a graveyard. Are you that fearful of the grave?"

Uthman replied:

"I heard the Messenger of God say:

'The grave is indeed the first stage in one's journey in the Hereafter. If a deceased one is saved from torments of the grave, the next stages will be more relaxing. If one is not saved from torments of the grave, the coming stages will be more trying and troublesome.'"

Uthman added that the Messenger of God concluded by saying:

"I have not seen any scene as grievous as the grave."

His Connection with God the Almighty

When Uthman's house was sieged by rebels, his wife Naila yelled at them:

"Are you willing to kill Uthman? By God! Either kill him or not, but do you know that Uthman revives his night with a single *rak'at* of prayer and recites the whole Qur'an in that single *rak'at*?"

Another example of Uthman's connection with the Almighty is narrated by Uthman ibn Abdur Rahman at-Taymi:

> One day I intended to revive all my night in Ka'ba by praying at Maqam al-Ibrahim (the station of Abraham), and I started praying there after completing the night prayer. Some-one touched my shoulder with his hand when I was praying. After my salutation, I noticed that the man was Uthman. Beginning with chapter Fatiha, he completed his prayer by reading the whole Qur'an, made salutation, and left by taking his shoes. I do not know if he previously had made any other prayers.

Muhammad ibn Sirin of the *Tabi'un* (genera-tion of Muslims who have not seen the Prophet but had seen his Companions), said:

"Uthman used to revive his nights and recite the whole Qur'an in a single *rak'at*."

Uthman's Not Awakening His Attendant

Uthman was a monument of chastity, as well as a man of good manners. He woke up one night for ablution. He prepared his water himself, made his ablution, and performed his prayer.

"O Commander of the Faithful! Why did you not wake one of your attendants to help you?" asked a man near Uthman.

"I would not! The night rest is also their right and I have no right to break their rest," he replied.

Uthman's Visit of Abdullah ibn Mas'ud during His Sickness

Abdullah ibn Mas'ud became sick one day. Uthman loved him very much and visited him. The following conversation transpired?

"What is your illness?" asked Uthman.

"My sins," replied Abdullah ibn Mas'ud.

"What are you longing for?"

"The mercy of my Lord…"

"Do you want me to send you a doctor?"

"The doctor made me sick."

"Do you want me to send you some benevolence?"

"No, I do not need any benevolence!"

"The benevolence would go to your daughters," Uthman said.

"Are you fearful that my daughters will fall into poverty?" asked Abdullah ibn Mas'ud; he then added:

"No, I advised my daughters to read chapter Waqi'ah every night. I heard the Messenger of God saying, 'Whoever reads the chapter Waqi'ah never faces poverty'."

Abdullah ibn Mas'ud died in Medina in the 32nd year of the Hijra. In his will that he left with Abdullah ibn Zubayr, he requested that he should be burried in the cemetery of *Jannatul Baqi* near the Prophet's Mosque. Uthman performed the funeral prayer.

Footsteps of Revolt against Him

Uthman was a kind person and as gentle as a dove. He also was good to his relatives. Those who did not know him believed that he showed nepotism to his relatives by appointing them to government positions. This misperception created jealousy among low-minded and malicious people. Uthman met with his governors in order to address the jealousies. They decided to send those who were dissatisfied with Uthman to Mecca for *Hajj* and meet with them in Medina after *Hajj*. It was hoped that by doing so all of the issues could be resolved and the misunderstandings removed. Uthman explained that he was helping his son-in-law and his other relatives from his own wealth, but there were some people who did not find his explanations convincing. Blazes of mischief and unrest had not yet burned out. Several mischief-makers were stirring up trouble, as they did not see Abu Bakr and Umar acting in this manner when they were Caliphs. They sent Ali ibn Abi Talib as an envoy to Uthman to discuss these matters. Ali paid a visit to Caliph Uthman and conveyed to him what his opponents were saying.

Uthman and Ali had heated discussions over the matters in dispute and a solution to the opponents' complaints was not found. Uthman rushed to the Prophet's Mosque to make a speech. In his speech, Uthman explained that those who were gossiping about him were doing wrong and that they were opposing him for things which they did not oppose during the Caliphate of Umar. He replied to those who accused him of nepotism by appointing his relatives as governors that Umar had worked with them in the same capacity.

The head mischief-maker was Abdullah ibn Sab'a. He declared that he had become a Muslim, but he was travelling everywhere to stir up unrest. He believed that he would achieve his goal by causing strife among the people. Wherever he found a group of dissatisfied people, he encouraged them to make mischief. He confused the Muslims with baseless assertions, such as that like Jesus, Prophet Muhammad will also resurrect after his death. Not able to stir up trouble in Damascus, Abdullah ibn Sab'a moved to Egypt.

He spread rumors in Egypt by saying that "the Prophet bequeathed Ali as the Caliph after him. Ali is his trustee," in order to suggest that Uthman's Caliphate was unjust. Uthman's opponents were ready to exploit these false claims. Trivial matters became issues of monumental importance. Situations that could have been assessed by looking at the glass half full were assessed by looking at its empty half! A tragedy was brewing. But how it was going to happen and who were going to be its victims were unclear.

Rebels' Allegations for Justification of Their Siege of Uthman's House

When sieging Uthman's house, the opponents asserted several reasons to justify their actions, desiring to have legitimate grounds. Throughout history, the logic of rebellions has never changed. In all rebellions there is an effort to find excuses and to disguise the real intentions. The opponents' allegations and Uthman's responses are as follows:

First allegation: "The Prophet and his two Caliphs Abu Bakr and Umar performed the prayers at Arafat during *Hajj* both in the forms of *taqsir* (shortening *rak'ats* of prayers during travelling) and *jam' baynas salatayn*.[1] But you applied only *jam' baynas salatayn* and performed the prayers in four *rak'ats* without applying the *taqsir*."

Uthman's replied:

"If I had applied the *taqsir* in the prayers, the pilgrims who came from distant territories would

---

[1] *Jam' baynas salatayn*: Joining of several prayer times in which *Dhuhr* (noon prayer) and *Asr* (afternoon prayer) prayers are combined into one prayer and offered between noon and sunset, and *Maghrib* (sunset prayer) and *Isha'a* (night prayer) prayers are combined into one and offered between sunset and predawn.

think that the prayers should always be performed in the shortened form, i.e., in two *rak'ats*, and they would perform their prayers as shortened when they return home. I performed the prayers in the full (unshortened) form to prevent a wrong practice from spreading among Muslims."

Second allegation: "The Messenger of God and his two Caliphs Abu Bakr and Umar used to esteem and be grateful to Abu Dharr. But you neither esteem him nor are you grateful to him. Instead, you sent him to his village Rabaza."

"I sent Abu Dharr to his village Rabaza because he could not bear the transformation that the Muslim community was going through. By sending him to his village, I recalled what the Messenger of God had said about Abu Dharr. Moreover, Abu Dharr did not object to my decision."

Third allegation: "In the beginning, *zakat* (obligatory alms) was collected by the *zakat* collectors. But you have left the collection of *zakat* to the free will of property owners. Consequently, people have begun paying *zakat* according to their own desires."

Uthman explained that the Muslim community was going through a transformation process and that the *zakat* collectors sometimes treated the property owners harshly. He added that he left the people free to pay their *zakat* and hoped that they would voluntarily do so.

Fourth allegation: "You let those whom the Messenger of God expelled from Medina return."

Uthman replied:

"During his sickness that led to his death, I asked the Messenger of God to permit two persons to return to Medina, and he gave me permission. I also told this matter to both Abu Bakr and Umar. They requested a witness from me, but I had no witness. When I was elected Caliph, I allowed those two persons to return to Medina upon the previous permission of the Messenger of God. They had already repented and stopped befriending hypocrites and infidels."

Fifth allegation: "You committed nepotism by assigning your relatives to government positions. You also increased your kinsmen's sustenances. This caused dissidence in the Muslim community."

Uthman responded: "God had granted me much wealth and I gave to my relatives from my wealth. I never distributed anything to my relatives from the state treasury. I gave from the state treasury to people only as much as they deserved. Why should I change my rightful habits at this age?"

Sixth allegation: "You had the *mus'hafs* that were compiled by Abu Bakr and belonged to Companions burned and left only a few. You also destroyed whatever remained in the hands of Muslims as bones, woods, and etc. on which they had written whatever had been revealed from the Qur'an during the time of the Messenger of God. What are your excuses for these deeds?"

Uthman said: "I was told by leading Companions that disputes over the reading of the Qur'an had begun, which might result in new unrest and seditions among Muslims. By behaving so, I believe that I prevented such probable seditions in the future. And no Companion objected to my action then."

Seventh allegation: The rebels raised flimsy arguments to cast blame on Uthman. For example, they said, "During your Caliphate, Abu Bakr stood one step below where the Messenger of God stood on the *minbar* (pulpit). Similarly, during his Caliphate Umar stood one step below where Abu Bakr stood at the *minbar*. But you stand where the Messenger of God stood at the *minbar*."

Uthman replied: "If I kept doing what those two Caliphs did, then Muslims would have had to dig into the ground and make steps beneath the earth in order to obey such a practice in the course of time! Thus, I did not follow them."

Eighth allegation: "We used to graze our herds at *Jannatul Baqi*, but you have prohibited this. Why did you do so?"

"I prohibited people from grazing their herds at *Jannatul Baqi* in order to let herds of the state graze there," he replied.

The rebels used as an excuse even the stamp ring of the Messenger of God which Uthman dropped into a well. However, each time Uthman convinced them.

The rebels dispersed as Uthman gave them persuasive answers. Ali ibn Abi Talib also prevented them from creating uproar.

Observations of Our Mother
Umm Salama

Our mother Umm Salama was a sagacious and astute woman. During the days of the Treaty of Hudaybiya, the Prophet sacrificed his animals after consulting her, which resulted in his Companions following his lead. Below are her observations regarding this event:

> *When the people were preparing for prayers during the time of the Messenger of God, they concentrated so much that they did not even look around except at their place of prostration. Even after the passing away of the Messenger of God, when they were preparing for prayers, no one's eyes shifted from the place where they would touch their foreheads for prostration. Even during the Caliphates of Abu Bakr and Umar, if people intended to make prayer, none of them used to shift their eyes from facing the qibla (direction of Ka'ba). But, unfortunately, incitements arose during the Caliphate of Uthman, and people began to lose concentration and look around during their worship to that extent that anyone watching them from outside would suspect if they were really praying or not.*

His Last Sermon

Uthman went to the Prophet's Mosque without paying any attention to the rebels and led the prayers. He stated in his last sermon:

> O congregation! God has bestowed to you this worldly life in order for you to get prepared for and earn your life in the Hereafter, but not for your sticking to it. This mundane life will end one day. The real and eternal life is the life of the Hereafter. Lest the mortal and transitory one keep you busy and retain you from the real and eternal one. There is indeed an end for this worldly life. Beware duly of God, for bewaring of Him is a shield that protects you from mischief and is also a cause for your pleasing Him. Seek refuge in God, preserve your congregation, and do not divide yourselves.

Uthman then read these verses from the Qur'an:

> And hold fast all together to the rope of God, and never be divided. Remember God's favor upon you: you were once enemies, and He reconciled your hearts so that through His favor, you became like brothers. You stood on the brink of a pit of fire, and He delivered you from it. Thus, God makes His signs of truth clear to you that you may be guided (to the Straight Path in

all matters, and be steadfast on it. There must be among you a community calling to good, and enjoining and actively promoting what is right, and forbidding and trying to prevent evil (in appropriate ways). They are those who are the prosperous (Al Imran 3:103–104).

Rebels' Sieging of Uthman's House

Ali talked to the rebels and ensured their return to their homelands. However, they found a way out of their agreement and returned again to Medina, sieging Uthman's house. They demanded that Uthman resign as Caliph. Uthman kept going to and returning from the Prophet's Mosque without paying them any attention. Meanwhile, the rebellion intensified and the demands of the rebels[2] became too difficult to

---

2   "This new group that was formed under the name Kharijites ("seceders", literary "those who went out") separated themselves from mainstream Islam. They were a radical, reactionary group who set about creating an ideal society through violence." (*Ali*, by Resit Haylamaz, New Jersey: Tughra Books, 2011, p. 103).

"They declared all others who did not think like themselves—including the Companions of the Prophet— infidels. Although they apparently believed in Islam, their vision was narrow and deprived of sound thinking."

meet. They completely sieged Uthman's house and did not even permit the delivery of water. Although the unrest had reached a devastating level, no one thought of using the army to quell it. Umm Habiba, who was one of the wives of the Prophet attempted to take a pitcher of water to Uthman's house. But the rebels startled her mount and she fell off with the water pitcher in her hand. Uthman, who had purchased and endowed the Ruma water well for the Muslims in better days, had now become in need of a drop of water, as he was no longer able to leave his house. Some of the leading Companions started to guard the front of Uthman's house with their swords in order to protect him. However, this proved to be a futile attempt. Eventually, one of the rebels stealthily entered the house and martyred Uthman, bringing a ruin to his own life in the Hereafter. Uthman had long ago heard from the Messenger of God that he was going to be martyred.

When martyred, Uthman's *mus'haf* was open and he was reciting the Holy Qur'an with a sweet and touching tune. Uthman was kind of a person who had an insatiable desire for reciting the Holy Qur'an. Let us incline our ear to his words, which show his heart's fondness of the Qur'an:

> It is impossible to be satiated with words of our Lord, the Almighty, if our hearts are not polluted. No matter how long we would be together with Him, the Almighty, we would desire to be with Him even more. If I live a mere day in which I did not recite some from the Mus'haf, I would suppose that I had lived my worst day ever.

Pages of Uthman's *mus'haf* were extremely worn out from extensive usage.

During the siege, Uthman climbed up on his roof and looked down at the rebels who had sieged his house. Sahl ibn Hunayf said about this incident:

"During the days in which he became house-bound due to the siege of the mischief makers, Caliph Uthman looked at them from the roof of his house and heard them talking about killing him and then he told us:

'These men are obviously threatening me with death. Why are they trying to kill me? I indeed heard the Messenger of God say:

'It is not legitimate to kill any Muslim due to any reason other than these three wrongdoings: A man who has fornicated after having sexual intercourse under a rightful marriage is to be stoned to death; a person who wrongfully killed someone is killed; and a person who has apostatized after becoming Muslim is killed.'

I swear God that, neither during the Age of Ignorance nor after becoming Muslim, I did not fornicate, nor did I kill any Muslim, nor did not apostatize from the time I became Muslim until now."

Attitudes of the Companions During the Siege

Abu Hurayra recounts those days:

"I went to Uthman's house during the days of siege and told him:

'O Commander of the Believers! For us war has become *halal* (lawful) now.'

'O Abu Hurayra! Are you willing to kill everybody and me?', asked Uthman.

'No', I said.

'I swear God, if you kill even a single person, it is as though you killed all men', Uthman told me. Upon his words, I dropped the idea of fighting and did not unsheathe my sword."

Some of the Companions told Uthman:

"O Commander of the Believers! There is a group of people supporting you in your house. By God's help, fight against the rebels with them. If God wills, He may save you even with a lesser group of people than that one. Permit us to fight against them."

"I would like to make all those who wish to shed blood of himself or someone else because of me remember God's glory," replied Uthman.

Zayd ibn Thabit was among those who visited Uthman during the siege.

"O Uthman! The *Ansar* are at your door and saying that they can be *Ansarullah* (Helpers of God) again if Uthman wishes!" he told Uthman.

"As for fighting, no! I will never fight," replied Uthman.

About seven hundred people were around Uthman; and by God's permission and help, they might have easily been victorious over the rebels and chased them from Medina. Among them were such heroes of the Messenger of God as

Abdullah ibn Umar, Hasan ibn Ali ibn Abi Talib, and Abdullah ibn Zubayr.

Said ibn al-As was also among those who came to support Uthman.

"O Commander of the Believers! Until now, we have not fought against the rebels. They are offending us. Some are shooting arrows; some are throwing stones; and some are unsheathing their swords against us. Command us to fight against them," he said to Uthman.

"As for me, I swear by God, I do not want to fight them. If I had wanted to, I am optimistic that God would have saved us from them. I am leaving their punishment to God. I also am leaving to God the punishment of those who provoked them against me. We will all be gathered before our Lord one day. As for fighting, I swear by God that I will not order you to fight," responded Uthman.

Upon his response, Said ibn al-As said:

"I swear by God that from now on I shall never ask you about fighting anybody."

Later, he started fighting the rebels and kept fighting until he received a fatal wound to his head. Said ibn al-As had made a personal *ijtihad* (judgment based on the Qur'an and the *Sunna*) on the matter. Accordingly, we may conclude that Companions did not leave Uthman alone in this time of crisis.

His Dream and Patience

Towards the morning of the day in which he was martyred, Uthman saw God's Messenger in a dream. The two previous Caliphs, Abu Bakr and Umar, were next to him. Uthman was mentally and spiritually ready to be martyred. He had made ablution and was fasting that day. The Messenger of God told him:

"O Uthman! Would you not like to break your fast with us today?"

Would it be possible for a Companion of Uthman's caliber to say 'no' to such a proposal of the most beloved?[3]

"I do not want to tempt anyone," said Uthman.

---

[3] During the first quarter of the twentieth century, Iskilipli Mehmet Atif Khodja stopped writing his plea and ripped up his rough draft after seeing the Prophet in a similar dream. He was a Turkish Islamic scholar executed in the early days of the Turkish Republic for his opposition to the banning of the fez and turban, and mandatory wearing of hat as a headgear (d. 1926).

If he had wished, Uthman could have made sure that none of the rebels survived the siege. There were people waiting to attack the rebels on the slightest sign of Uthman. One may wonder why Uthman did not order them to attack.

Uthman presumably hoped that the rebels would eventually cease their siege, as he did not believe that a Muslim would act in such hostility to a Companion of the Prophet. However, mischief-making and cursed souls had taken the stage.

When martyred, Uthman was reciting the Holy Qur'an. He used to finish one complete reading of the Qur'an in a week. He was reading verses 169–173 of the chapter Al Imran:

> *Do not think at all of those killed in God's cause as dead. Rather, they are alive, with their Lord, they have their sustenance. Rejoicing in what God has granted them out of His bounty and joyful in the glad tidings for those left behind who have not yet joined them that (in the event of martyrdom) they will have no fear, nor will they grieve. They are joyful in the glad tidings of God's blessing and bounty (that He has prepared for the martyrs), and in (the promise) that God never leaves to waste the reward of the believers. Those who responded*

to the call of God and the Messenger after the
hurt had befallen them – for all those of them
who persevered in doing good, aware that God
was seeing them, and acted in reverence for
God and piety, there is a tremendous reward.
Those to whom some people said: "Look, those
people have gathered against you, therefore be
fearful of them." But it increased them only in
faith, and they responded: "God is sufficient
for us; how excellent a Guardian He is!

Only his wife Naila was with Uthman when he was martyred.

The Position of Those Who Sieged His House

A man named Abu Kilaba narrated an event he witnessed in Damascus:

"I travelled to Damascus with some of my friends. We heard the voice of a man whose hands and feet were chopped off by his wrists; his face was severely disfigured and he was blind."

"What happened to you?" I asked the man.

He replied:

"I was one of those who entered the house of Uthman in that *yawmud dar* (the day in which Uthman's house was sieged by the rebels). Uthman's wife began screaming as I approached him and I violently slapped her face. When Uthman saw my slap, he said 'Shame on you! May God chop your hands and feet off and make you blind. And your end be Hell.' I cannot tell you how deeply shocked I was in that moment. And as you can see now, all Uthman wished has happened to me. My hands and feet are chopped off. And I don't know what I shall do if I end up in Hell. That's why I have been screaming and crying."

"I too said to the man 'Shame on you' and left him," Abu Kilaba concluded.

The grave of Uthman ibn Affan in the Jannatul Baqi Cemetery

APPENDICES

Pioneering Acts of Uthman

Uthman was the first man who;

1. divided the lands into plots

2. allocated the woods and groves for public usage

3. did not raise his voice when reciting *takbir* (proclamation of the greatness of God) during leading prayers

4. spread perfumes in the Prophet's Mosque

5. ordered the call of *adhan* (invitation) before *Juma* (Friday) prayer

6. started paying salaries to *muazzins* (those who lead the call to prayers)

7. gave a sermon before the prayers of the *Eid ul-Fitr* (Festival of the Fast Breaking) and the *Eid al-Adha* (Festival of the Sacrifice)

8. authorized everybody to determine their *zakat* (obligatory alms) by themselves

9. started a security system similar to police organization

10. built a special place for prayers in the Prophet's Mosque to prevent an assault similar to that assault inflicted on Umar

11. was Caliph during the first *fitna* (sedition and unrest) among the *ummah*

12. migrated with his wife

The Hadiths Narrated by Uthman

Uthman was one of those Companions who narrated hadiths from the Messenger of God. Below are several of the hadiths narrated by him:

1. I heard God's Messenger say: "Whoever performs ablution and does it well, goes to mosque and offers prayer, his (sins) during the period from that prayer to the next would be pardoned by God."

2. I heard God's Messenger say: "A man in *ihram* (the state of sacred purity the Muslim faithful must enter before conducting the pilgrimage to Mecca) should not give someone in marriage or get married or get betrothed."

3. I heard God's Messenger say: "The most valued of you is the one who learns and teaches the Qur'an."

4. I heard God's Messenger say: "Whoever performs ablution as ordered by God the Almighty, and offers the *fard* (obligatory) prayers with this ablution, this deed will be *kaffara* (a thing that wipes out wrongdoings) for the sins he did between the prayers."

5. I heard God's Messenger say: "Whoever offers *Isha'a* (night prayer) and *Fajr* (dawn prayer) in congregation, it is as if he spent his entire night in worship."

6. One day Uthman asked for some water for ablution. He began performing ablution, by putting water into his mouth, snuffing water into his nose, dashing water on his face three times, washing his arms to the elbows three times, rubbing his head with water, and washing his feet to the ankles. Upon completing ablution, he smiled and asked those around him:

"Are you not going to ask me what makes me smile?"

"Why did you smile, O Commander of the Believers?" they asked.

Uthman replied:

"I saw God's Messenger asked for water for ablution around here one day. After he performed ablution as I did now, he smiled and asked:

'Are you not going to ask me what made me smile?'

His beloved Companions asked:

'What made you smile, O God's Messenger?'

He replied: 'If a servant asks for water for ablution and starts performing it, all the sins he has committed with his face are forgiven. When he washes his arms, the same applies. When he rubs his head, the same applies. When he washes his feet, the same applies.'"

7. Uthman narrates: "Upon completing the burial of a deceased, God's Messenger used to stay besides the grave and say:

'Ask God's mercy and pray for firmness for your brother as he will be called to account now.'"

8. Uthman narrates: "God's Messenger performed ablution by washing his body parts three times and would say:

'This is the ablution of me, the Prophets before me, and Abraham.'"

9. Uthman narrates: "I heard God's Messenger say:

'Whoever builds a mosque for God's good pleasure, God builds a mosque twice the size of it in Paradise.'"

10. I heard God's Messenger say:

"Nothing can cause harm to a believer who says the prayer 'In the name of God with whose name nothing can cause harm in the earth and in the heaven. And He is All-Hearing, All-Knowing' three times in every morning and every evening of the day."

As Abu Hurayra narrated, God's Messenger said:

"Modesty is a branch of faith and Uthman is the most modest of my *ummah*."

Eloquent Sayings Attributed to Uthman

Uthman could speak quite eloquently, for example:

"Ten things are deemed to have lost.

First: The scholar who is not asked a question,

Second: Knowledge which is not put into practice,

Third: An idea that is not accepted,

Fourth: A weapon which is not used,

Fifth: A mosque in which no prayer is made,

Sixth: The Qur'an which is not recited,

Seventh: Property which is not distributed to the needy as charity,

Eighth: A mount which is not ridden,

Ninth: Learning only for worldly purposes,

Tent: A life in which no preparation is made for the journey to the Hereafter."

A person who excelled in his education and training under the guidance of God's Messenger could only speak this way.

Below is another example of Uthman's eloquence:

"The Almighty God rewards the following nine beneficences to those who regularly make prayers five times without any disruption:

First: God loves those persons,

Second: God bestows health and wellbeing to their bodies,

Third: The angels protect and pray for forgiveness of their sins and bad deeds,

Fourth: Their houses become fruitful,

Fifth: They have a light which is bestowed only to the righteous people on earth,

Sixth: God renders soft the heart of those who make prayer,

Seventh: They pass the *Sirat* (the bridge which every person must pass on the Day of Resurrection to enter Paradise) with lightning speed,

Eighth: God protects them from Hell,

Ninth: They hang together with those who enjoy the privileges of the verse, '…and they will have no fear, nor will they grieve' (Baqara 2:62)."